# Poems for Wyatt
## An Archive of Infant Loss and Recurrent Pregnancy Loss

# By Mandy Kelso

Poems written in the days before and following infant loss, and the twelve miscarriages that preceded and followed.

This book is dedicated to
Dr. Shilpi Mehta-Lee,
Dr. Zev Williams,
My husband, Robbie,
My daughter, Reilly,
and my beloved son, Wyatt.

Thank you for giving me hope
When I could no longer find it
On my own.

# Poems for Wyatt

# Preface Poem

1.7.2014
Coming to Terms

What is the term? And who said it?
My body is *a temple*
But here in this temple
Paper gowns
Sunlight resting on sterile things
Masked strangers, whose voices drown
In whispers about the
End of terms.
What was the term?
Blighted? Marred?
These were Your terms,
I come to them in this sterile room
I sit with them in Your sunlight
On the soaked paper gown
Your terms for this temple where things go to die
The strangers You gave me—
Masked mouths with no *why*.

I punch bulbs the size of fists into the snow.
Tulips will grow, bright and festive come spring;
Just beneath the earth, all in a row.
Tidy. In time. I know.
These are Your terms.
Germinate. Terminate.
Terminal. Terms of Endearment.
Terms of Engagement.
Preterm. End of term. Post.
A time, a term for every time, for every season
A name for Your terms—a *time-term* for Your reasons
If I could just bear them—
*Bright and festive come spring*

Preterm. End of term.
Post.
More gorgeous than most;
Pristine white gown turned to paper
Soaked red bulbs all in a row.
These are the only promises You bring.

I come to You with my fists full of tulips.
I come to You with my open temple,
This time, my mouth is still.
Loss has washed me silent;
And I sit hopeful with You,
In Your sunlight
While You offer what terms You will.

# Neonatal Stay

4.1.15
Stay

Let us peer through this tenuous opening
The way bloody, juicy, soft
I will cover for you when it is time,
I will tell you to run, son
But until then, let us peek around the corner
Let us play in the water
Let us take our time.

My body has always been anxious.
Each stretch of muscle trained to run,
Instinctively it follows the wrong instincts
Duck when I should hunt
Hunt when I should tend
Tend when I should shun
Shun when I should mend.

I want better for you. Let us take our time.

You have learned to punch and kick.
And you have learned to smile.
Learn to stay. To hang on.
I'm sorry you have to learn so early what I have learned so
late.
Hiccup your way through strengthening lungs,
Let your heart accelerate
To the cadence of words said aloud
Echoing through watery speakers
I am talking to you, loving you, wanting you to hear my
message,
Wanting you to play with me
To enjoy it, take it easy, our time so close together on this
earth is short
By any measure,
Each day a gift, a lovely path

Let's meander
Through the thinning muscle that separates their world
from ours
Soon enough it will be too thin,
Soon enough it will break,
So let us take our time
With it still wrapped thick and blanketing
Your heart to mine.

4.2.15
Our Lives

These are our lives
Full of insects that crawl up leaves
Into the cups of Easter Lilies
Full of slow-turning blooms
Sometimes unfolding in white rooms
Day by day, we water them
Paint them
With whatever we have at our disposal
Which is sometimes an army of hyacinth
Sometimes only our own untamed blood

Stay here in our lives in the moment
Which will never be the same, can never be undone
So I flick on a tune that reminds us to slow down
Harken in our sunny room, to the
Smell of hyacinth, make our promises to remark on
The sparkling view from where we are,
The metal-corded bridge piecing worlds together
Across abundant waters
The richness of chocolate and softness of lathered soap
The small graces we are here allotted
God's soft kisses atop the heads of lives carried
Through quiet rooms, to help us bear the secrets
That the water, the flowers, the blood
Stitch together, seemingly without us.

We make our earnest and heartfelt requests
Throw them up like pollen, and sometimes like paint
We conjure our own secrets,
Which catch on the legs of moving things
And make their way towards the delicate folds of carpel
To leave our mark, our own stain of color
On lives stitched together, seemingly without us.

4.3.15
Nights

Nights are long corridors
With some doors opened, some closed,
With unhurried footsteps
And the sighs of hinges;
Each of which you can't but faintly hope
Might signify the morning.

# The Fact

Wyatt Wolfgang Kelso born April 3, 2015, died April 4, 2015.

# Journey

4.5.15
Ashes

Mirror of genetics
Or the Universe's own immaculate tessellation
The way you fit into my chest
The yin yang of your heart feeding mine, you nuzzled
against my breast
Just the right size, no space spared,
Your father's arms around us
Unit of love, three chests shared
As petals protect the seed,
Breathing, beating, protecting as One Being,
Single surge of life bursting forth
As nature had designed, the three of us, you at the core
Of this family,
Our family.
Having known this miraculous Oneness,
Tell me what is left in our chests now that you are gone
Tell me what of the three of us
Has not turned to ashes?

4.6.15
Milk

My milk came in today.
My body refuses to believe we've lost our son.
I hold ice packs and cabbage leaves to my chest
Instead of my warm boy
But my body cannot comprehend our loss.
We cannot comprehend our loss.

4.7.15
Home Today

Home today
Empty belly, empty bassinet
Stitched up womb stuffed with Percocet
My strong husband in a pile on our bed
Cold cabbage leaves pressed to aching breasts
Our son's ashes on their way.

My friends and family say
We are thinking of you,
Tell us what you want us to do
Tell us, we are grieving for you,
But I have no words, only pictures
Of his last moments in our arms
No requests, except make it all untrue.

4.7.15
Mine

Upon the hour, prayers stream in
And I feel the soft tug of comfort
Nudging at my edges, words of love
Prying grief from my fists
But I cannot let go of it.

This breathlessness is mine to keep
I would not give it up any more than I would give up
My love for him, his precious body,
His perfect spirit—mine to weep
The warmth of his little furrowed brow
When they handed him to me
His legs still, unmoving under the swaddling blanket
My friends say they would carry this for me if they could
But I carried him in this body—the weight of us were one
A balance that could not be unhanded
Re-allocated or undone
His bluing body light as a feather
My heart heavy as a stone.

4.7.17
Emily, the Social Worker Called

Emily, the social worker, called
But I don't want to talk
I want to punch and kick
But I can barely walk
I want to beat my chest and tear my clothes to shreds
But my breasts have become
Knotted lumps, a stone cage,
Bracing my heart from my fists' rage
My hands grip-less, I sob from a heap in my bed instead.
What is the Universe protecting by weakening me so?
Itself or me? Answer me that, Emily.
I want to know
Why the Universe cut from my belly what I loved most
Why it left me too weak to intervene as it turned him to a
ghost
Too weak to stand, why I had to sit
Burying him in my tears, witnessing all of it
Offering him only the hollowed torso, where he should
have been, safe and warm,
I don't want to talk to you, there's nothing to sort— I want
him back.
I want answers
And you can't give me that.

4.9.15
Unraveling

The Universe is now undoing
All the work that we had done.
My body, once filled with your wonder
Is a sullied, unmade bed

I miss your magic.

I hate my body without you.
I hate it for not keeping you longer.
What would it have taken to keep you one more week?
One more week, and a lifetime?
Why should I heal while you sit in ashes at my bedside
All that we made undone?

4.10.15
At Sea

My husband looks at me
His face a ship at sea
He says, "I need you."
Our eyes are anchor-less,
Or maybe it's just me.
I'm not ready to go back to the shore,
Where our loved ones are waiting to grab us and hold us to
the land.
I don't want to remember what's there—
What they know and want me to remember.
I want no more of the seasons.

4.10.15
Need

Today I told my husband that I wanted to eat our son's
ashes.
He belongs inside of me until spring, when he can survive
without me.
I've read of pregnant women eating charcoal and dirt;
Doctors shake their heads and say what she's really craving
is iron.

What would they say if I gulped down his ashes?
What would they say my blood was craving then?
Could they name the profound deficiencies everywhere
inside me
That only what's left of him could fill?

4.11.17
The Day

It was a sad day when our friends finally came
And I had to admit to them that you were gone;
They said they didn't need reasons,
But we all did, we all wanted to know
About your soft hair, the heavenly smell of you,
The lungs that pushed so hard for so long
Then tired unexpectedly in the night,
Your fighting heart, enlarged from all the struggle.
We did not want this suffering for you.
We did not want to admit that we had taken the miracle of
your life for granted.
So many miracles happen these days, we thought;
The car seat parked by the door.

4.14.15
Ruckus

My friends move like a single hundred-handed giant
Where they roam, they leave things shinier, cleaner, fuller
than when they came.
Like a single body, they move in through the front door,
hoisting bags, flowers, books,
Pots descend from latches, washing machines hum;
They gather everything in their wake, move it from hand to
hand,
One lathering, one scrubbing, one polishing, until things
pop back into place,
Gleaming from fresh attention.
The cats get tickled behind the ears. The dead leaves on the
lawn march into bags.
Sometimes I catch myself laughing, tasting the delicious
foods they pull endlessly out of their aprons;
And I wonder if I'm ready for all the ruckus of love.

They see my face and tell me they are here to worry about
all that.
They tell me all I have to do is breathe—I don't even have
to move.
So that is what I do
As they pass me from hand to hand
Shining me up one by one with their warm shirtsleeves,
repetitive brush strokes
They kiss my nose and tell me which foot goes first
Where they've stashed the leftovers; how to heat them up
They remind me how to chew
A hundred hands holding me together,
Assuring me that I will gleam again soon.

And for a moment after the door has shut behind them,
before the house settles back into its stunned silence
We all believe it could be true.

4.18.15
Haiku

Some trees still won't turn
Limbs tremble, distrusting sun
Winter robbed us all.

4.18.15
Your Name

I know why God named each creature, one by one
It was the promise made, the final guarantee of existence
Of love.
And so we named you. As if to etch in early the certainty of
your existence.
How we love your name, Wyatt,
And each small movement, each day of your growth
assigned to it.

We introduced you early,
That we could all begin to love you,
Calling out your name in our prayers,
Delighting in the way you changed me,
The introductions over, we made you family,
We knit you into us, as if coming from my body may not be
enough,
We etched you into the Universe under the family name,
Bound you to our brothers, your namesake,
Called upon fierce and wild spirits to protect you,
It was our greatest act of love, we thought, to share your
name with the world
That others could begin to love you with us—
That through this great love, we could keep you.

We named you and we thought we could make you ours.
But God knew who you were before we did,
And He need only call upon you once
To make you His again;
Our voices forever trailing after
Calling and calling your name.

4.24.15
Too Much

I don't know what color your eyes were
They were shut when they handed you to me
Your pinkish brow still warm and balmy
After so much work,
You looked like you were drifting into sleep,
Your heart rate gently falling
So tired—it was all too much
Too much to ask of someone so little and so new
Unfair of me to ask of you
To keep on trying
When I had not given you enough time to prepare
Unfair of me to ask of you, when you had not had enough
time to grow,
You looked like you were drifting into sleep,
Too much of me to ask of you
Not to go.

It doesn't say on your birth certificate or your death
certificate
What color your eyes were:
Just two time stamps, nineteen hours and twenty-six
minutes apart
Your gorgeous name framed on two royal blue papers;
The lost color of your eyes
Drawing black curtains over my heart.

4.24.15
The Seasons

You were not due till long after the cherry blossoms came
Long after spring bulbs had bloomed
And summer too
End of June, I would come to you
And introduce you to the seasons.
Always, my son, we wait for the seasons.

I asked your father what happens if we plant a bulb too
soon?
A fall bulb, planted in May, for example…
He said you can't plant what is already in bloom,
Wait, wait, for the seasons.

Perhaps you are too much like me,
Impatient. Eager. Perhaps it was not you but me,
Being impatient. Eager.
Perhaps I never had faith in the seasons.

4.28.15
Morning

Sorrow nudges me awake
The sky no longer shares its secrets with me.
There are no hidden messages in the gardenia.
The world has become mute, dumb.
Except for his name, which echoes on and on.

4.29.15
The Barren One

I cannot go home
And be the Barren One.
The Careless One.
My head bowed to my mother
Having lost many now
In a family that never failed to fruit.

I cannot be the Fallow One,
My grandmother's many daughters and sons
Heirloomed, toes deep in the rich soil that brings them joy
Generation after generation
I say I have tended, I swear it,
My tears buried in my hands,
Mother, I have tried—
I curse the rocky earth beneath me,
The weeds that will not leave me,
The parched and cloudless sky.

5.1.15
This House

Littered with the details of grief
The kitchen sink
Still waiting for its tiny bather
The cushioned chair framed against the bird-curtained
window
Silently perched for a story,
Drawers of precious
Fabrics waiting for your skin
How do we re-begin?

How do we recalculate our lives without you?
What do we do with cradles that are meant to hold you?
Or the bright books on the shelves
Whose every first page joyously bears your name?
How can any room in this house ever be the same?

5.4.15
Anniversary Day

I pad around this great house
Nudging at the motionless heap of my loss
Like a dog would a dead master;
But all that once was warm, familiar, and roaming
Has stiffened into the frigid and alien form before me.
I paw at it desperately.
But it is unmovable.

5.13.15
For My Husband, Our Heads Bent Low

There is a tree up on the crest of a mountain
Do you remember it?
Bent and twisted pine reposed at the top of the Nears?
We sat one day, I painted it.
You drew me to you, kissed my ear.

We called it Ours.
I said I was Yours,
When you bent your knee there beneath it
Offering the Fullest Forever;
I said yes then, and I still believe it.

We have made family of the crooked pine,
Clinging to the side of the mountain
Bones bent from blows dealt by time
Roots deep in search of fountain
Growing outward when we must, and then up,
Searching first for sky or wind
Learning to trust each untamed gust
To carry our seed again
Into the rocky, shaded valley,
We grow on clinging, bereft of our cones
However, however we can.

What can be said of our twisted pine
Except that we both sensed the divine
The day that we first found it?
Our Fullest Forever has bent us low
But hands clasped, we take each blow
And let our love grow strong around it.

5.14.15
Reset

Red reset
recycled bloodlet
my baby carved out of me
The only language my womb
knows how to use
shakes loose
the blood of our clotted roots
The veins red and blue
sheds, forgets
What remains
of all promises of our making
all that we built together
Red, the pool of our unity
the too-early ejection of my most prized creation
the most precious part of me
Red, the heart that reached its tendrils all around him
Promises to him, broken, cleaved
Red, the bed, the vile reset
That took his heart from me.

5.14.15
Beasts

I move my hands
Folding white shirts
Refilling the ice trays
Scraping food from dishes
Dumbly, they drag me through each mundane task
And I wonder why and how they can do that without me?
I wonder what feeds these beasts
Now that my heart is dead?

5.29.15
Not Enough

What do I do with all the room I had made for you?
Thousands of lilies bloom
Liatrus, peeking blue
I soak them in hopes they will fill me of you
But they scarcely cling to a corner.
I have room left over.

5.29.15
Mother of Lilies

I have become a demanding mother: "Tell me you love
me!" "Prove to me that you are still here with me!"
The mother I never wanted to be.
Demanding loyalty, proof, when in truth, I hope that you
are set free
The lilies unfold and I think I am holding you
Crouching down in the field of them
My chest aching just to reach you
The petals fall when I barely touch them and I feel that I
have broken everything that I have ever loved
The red beetles munch on your leaves and I kill them one
by one but cannot ever seem to protect you
The long list of my failures transmitting through their
elusive antennae
I am the mother of lilies now
To care for them and watch them grow my new concern
I am a critical mother
Where is the random kick of your legs when you hear my
voice?
Or the tiny toes that curl and uncurl as you're dreaming?
Or that soft spot right under your chin that I long to nuzzle?
What of these things does a mother of lilies know
But still I demand them of you
As I search your spirit in the fields
I am constantly asking you questions, wanting you to
comfort me through their colors
The roles reversed as I swore they would not—I am the
child looking for the hand to hold
Should your absence be any excuse? Should I hover, over
and over, trying to keep you close, pulled to me, rather than
roaming, growing, in worlds I cannot see?
No.
Son, please forgive me.
I am not the mother I meant to be.

7.21.15
Back At Work

I can't stand the steel-coated conference tables
The right angles that remember nothing
I can't breathe, ghosts kick inside me
They summon my animal self
Ears perked up, I hear everything everything
Sitting in this chair, in this boardroom
The fans whirring against suit collars
The pens clicking in and out, hum of voices back and forth
While my mind pads through like a wolf in the forest
Sniffing out the thing that's out of place
The bent blade of grass misaligned with my memory
What is amiss in this slick room with straight edges
Tucked away from the natural world where my mind roams
I can't feel the lilies' heavy heads against my knees,
We are so far away
There is no trace, no memory
Of warm spots made inside folded arms
Or the heavenly scents that accompany small curves
Or the body that leans into the breeze
Wondering if it will ever carry a baby's cry.

9.16.15
Live Oak

Old oak, Live Oak, your gnarly skin dressed in velvet
gowns
of verdant resurrection ferns
Old Queen,
Tell me
about the relative survival of things.

Tell me what you have seen
these five hundred years
of humans who have died in nicks and slices
their spirits rubbed out of them
one goodbye at a time

You seem to me a miracle.

I am not the first to sob in your lap
Or hide myself beneath your sleeves
Who am I to complain of an empty core?
What are my tears to the blood you have soaked up?
I have lost a son, but you have lost many
holding their forgotten bones to you deep in the earth
holding them still in your subterranean embrace
you show me your scarred bark
burled from surviving siege after siege
I ask how you can tolerate the moss that clings to your
limbs like an insistent toddler
Even while you cradle the bones of your many dead
children
"It is the way," I hear you say,
"Let the creatures of the sky and earth see the sun crowning
your head
But hold him dear always, let him be your roots."

9.26.15
Not ready for Autumn

Don't fall.
I'm not ready for your golds and reds.
I sit too much with scarcity, arms and head
Though you have offered it all.

I have had every color you could afford
You've pulled astonishing pinks and yellows
Of your magical accord
From the earthen brown
Surrounded me in the aromatic elixirs
You've summoned from the ground
And still I need need need.
What will I do without your leaves?

I am not faithful enough to believe
That everything that I still love
Grows steadfastly,
No sign of life
No promise

That you live yet beneath the ground.

9.29.15
Blood Moon

The moon is red-faced and swollen
Revolution by revolution we have come to this
A skirting about the tipped ellipsis
A tiptoeing year after year
Until today, the coldest day
The day we admit that we have cut the moon

11.5.15
The marriage

The rules of love are confusing
Do you have to be lovely to be loved?
As summer pulls its bangs away
looks at you with naked eyes
leaves you in demise
when you leave that door
Everyone I've ever loved leaves and more,
And I am angry fighting shadows bigger than us
I don't expect you to understand
you who have been treasured
coddled
who even today takes love for granted.

This is an uneasy love, scattered
It cycles
One day, you, on your page of grief,
Me on mine of reprieve
The next day the places exchanged
Never landing the same
I am batted between the gloves of shock and anger
A need to run and a need to cling
I am the ingredient that turns good to bad
Sweet beginnings that end with a sting
The unlovely one
I am sorry
It is too much all of this.

Go be lovely any way you can
because even if I wanted to fix this,
I don't know how.
Cursed are we and everything
that stands between us and the sun.

11.7.15
The Weight

What is there to do but wait
For time to wear itself out on us
As we know it must
For a day that doesn't sulk around the corners of rooms
or tear up at the edges of morning or dusk
when the light touches everything that was supposed to be
different?

What is grief
But love that lingers still in rooms
Or memories that refuse to be pushed through
of a hope that turned hard, that crushed you
While you were laying
Sweetly in its palm?

12.30.15
Try Again

The day he died, I said we'll try again
Because I had broken him and had been caught
Because I had failed again
And needed to make it up to everyone
Because my son
I wanted him to live again and I didn't know how to make
him
He couldn't breathe
And I didn't know how to help him
I couldn't
I had come too late
I didn't know what to say
I couldn't believe
The silence of his hands
I said I'll fix it I swear
We'll try again
Because everything everything had broken
And I had broken it
And I didn't know how to make it right.

And now it is time to try again like I said I would.
To open again the womb that gave him its best but still
came up short.
I want to fix it.
But the memory of his head
His sweet and perfect head
His hands, immaculate even in their stillness,
Lie heavy
Lie sweetly
Lie incomprehensibly
On my chest
Insisting that what was broken
Can never be fixed again
Insisting that what was broken—what is broken—

Is, was always,
Me.

I said, we'll try again, I swear it,
And now I have to do it,
Because we are only ever truly broken,
—*I hold his memory tightly to my chest*—
I am only broken
—*My lungs tighten with grief*—
If I don't keep moving forward,
—*It can't be fixed*—
But *I* can
Try again.

3.16.16
Despised Guest

Spring has shown up like a guest who was thrown out of
the house ages ago.
My husband and I are speechless at her shameless bravado
knocking at our door
She has decorated the trees with heavy glistening buds
Has nudged the bulbs awake, shined up some of their color
She knows how much I love purples and greens and I think
she is trying to soften me up
For the Great Forgive.

But we remember her treachery:
Showing up last year after we had survived the long winter
Distracting us with the smells of hyacinth and the pink
promises of tulips in bloom
We were looking the other way
When she snuck on dappled feet into the room
Where my son lay to steal him.
The cherry trees began to burst that day, above rows of
screaming daffodils, angel white magnolia
As if to say
You may have everything this spring
A basketful of obscene colors
In which to bury him.

She's out on the porch right now, callous bitch.
She's not even apologizing,
Just glowing and waiting.

We hiss through the door
Were we not clear enough in our ask?
If you loved us, why did you sabotage us?
Why did you make us fools?

But she says nothing.

47

Just lays at our feet again her basket
Of obscene colors and stillness.

3.29.16
By the stone

I waited around the stone
Took my meals around the tomb of whatever was left of
you—
The receiving blanket
The tiny socks.
How recently you were with me.

You were born on Good Friday
And left me the day before Easter
So I waited there for our miracle
For you to return to the crib we had built you
I didn't know how it would work
Your body had become ashes
But everyone kept saying "have faith"
And I had faith.

It has been a year and the lilies we planted for you have had
little babies of their own:
Small bulbettes cling to their mommas beneath the earth
And they will all rise together—
Little blooming families.

I am and I am not their mother.
I am yours
And your many brothers and sisters laid in the ground.
They say I must resurrect. I am the one that must live again.
Small green leaves point like fingers to the sky where you
are.
How can I come back?
Why should I?
When you didn't—
When I waited by the stone?

6.28.16
What is there

I want to write a poem that is not about a flower
Or my own blood
Or the name that clinks away in me like so many coins
slapping the water of a fountain
What is there then?

There's the lazy sound of the Spanish guitar
And the waxy oil pastel squishing around my pressed
fingers
While I force upon the canvas it's sloppy, uncommitted
kiss.

7.24.16
For the Sleepless

The night stars stare back at me
Matter-of-factly
We share this still porch
We collect the night together.

I am tired of remembering the tangible things
And intangible things
That cling to my mouth
Crumbs that I cannot wipe away

I don't want to remember their testament to brimming days,
ripe and full
While I sit here dried up and brittle inside
Forever lost to the eloquent hymn of him
The nights now mute, cradling only a silenced orchestra of
blank-eyed stars
They stare back at me
Dried and brittle
A shriveled gourd begging from my stiff porch
This, my rattling song

10.4.16
The Circle

Here is my song for the mothers who don't bring home
babies
After the labor, after the many months
Who lie in rooms with other mothers, babbling on
Until they separate you from the throng
Give you your own room just for the night
Where you can howl in privacy
The stains of your c-section still soaking the pads
In the long night that turns into the long year
The long life
Without your baby.

The sky will lose some color, yes,
As milk pours and pours from your breast
Looking for the small mouth, the small miraculous mouth
That was meant for you
Tiny, round, never to be found.

They'll give you a box of your baby's things
Footprints, snippets of hair,
Down at the bottom will be a prayer
And directions for the nearest support group
Where a social worker named Al will sit in a circle
Like a piercing, the couples looping from his left to his
right
Glistening with tears
on the ear of some cold church basement

Come find us, the mothers like me and you,
Come find us if it is all you do—and we will sit with you
quietly.
We will say your baby's name with you over and over
We will whisper with you, grieving mothers

We will circle you with our love and curse whatever you
need us to:
Tuesdays, spring, the too-early mornings, the too-late
goodbyes,
Hope.  We'll curse it all in the name of your Loss
Because we know how much you need it.

Wander and we'll tell you that's ok, we'll hold a spot for
you
In our strange and loving club.  We'll talk to the dead in
every field together as long and often as we must.

Here's my song for you, now that I've been down that road
a bit
Every moment looking back asking "Can this really be my
life?"
They will say have another baby, or a kitten
But sometimes you can't do even that
Paralyzed by the silence of the crib you built for your baby.

But keep walking.  We're here.
Because one day, far far far from the day you left that
hospital empty-armed
You'll venture out into a starry sky, your cracked feet
beneath you
Your tongue will be tired of curses
Your breasts will settle back into your chest
Your eyes will be looking for nothing
The sky will unravel before you in its Fullness
Inexplicable light will dance down on you,
And I swear to you Sweet Sister,
Wonder will make you whole again.

11.2.16
The Hard Winter

The hardest winter lasted from October to April
I remember because my feet kept slipping on the ice month
after month
The new weight of my growing belly throwing me off
balance
The heat inside me like a hearth keeping my baby and me
warm
our summoned antidote to the bitter cold of six-foot snows.
The fruit trees in my yard felt it too,
Stuck in their icy homes
Waiting out the longer-than-usual months
If we could just make it,
The promise of the harvest of our lifetimes hung at the end
of all that packed-in ice,
And sure enough, come Spring that year, the buds became
flowers, which quickly turned to fruit
All but mine.

The following winter was mild, errant even.
None of us bore fruit.
Even the peach tree forewent it's lovemaking to grow extra
leaves instead.
The flowers were apologetic, stunted, and irregular,
Like my own footsteps, unsure on the wet grass
As my body ran through one blunted promise after another.
The sicknesses that plagued us late in fall simply grew over
the mild winter
With no harshness to kill them off while we survived to be
stronger
And one by one we watched them take their toll on
whatever flowers we managed to bear.

They say we are headed for another hard winter.

Already the ground has iced over and the grass has turned in its green.

I can taste the sweet pears, the peaches, the cherries on the other side of it, and wonder what it will bring to me.

11.15.16
Humiliated

Hope is a train ticket you store in the back of your wallet
Some days you take it out and examine it
Contemplating the expiration date
Wondering how many times the lady behind the window
will exchange it
Before the day she finally says "I'm sorry but..."—
Her voice 50% fed-up, 50% ridicule

Sometimes I want to tear the ticket up in disgust
Humiliated that I even bought it
Thinking they'd finally tell me what platform, what
departure
Wondering what I could have bought instead
What I could have seen

But if I tore it up
Would I ache for that empty slot
Would I keep remnants somewhere else?
Submarined where no one can see? Resurfacing only in
dreams?

Would I set up camp at the station
Rueful of every passerby, envious of the ticket they hold so
surely in their hands?

12.6.16
Hope

I'm not the only one like me
Who has heard the heart's fluttering
Turn into the fluttering of wings
Who imagines grapes plump with seed
Emerging triumphant from the strangling weeds
Who believes in the egg tooth's tapping
With impossible strength
The unlikely unwrapping
At the day's long length
The wings hard flapping
Gulping the wind beneath

12.21.16
The Odd Beat

The more I hear the slow, the odd beat
The more I want you to keep beating
We are all odd, are we not?
We all fall out of tune,
I hope outside the lines
The days and weeks the doctors prescribe
Before the beat slows to stop
Before they declare demise
You jump outside the lines
Wander off dancing to your odd beat
While I miss you, while my feet ghost dance,
I love you *Little Odd Beat*.

12.22.18
Outside the Lines

Sometimes we cry in public places
Trapped inside train windows
Defeated, beaten by the odds

I get in trouble hoping outside the lines
I get in trouble because I don't see the lines

12.21.16
Surrender by the Christmas Tree

There is tinsel on the tree and I see it reflecting the room
back at me in a wiry glow
Life is going on with me in tow
Too tired, to fight,
I let it take me where it wants to go.


If I think about your little feet, I say to myself, you don't
have to worry about that any more.
The Universe is watching now.
You won't accidentally pull anything off the tree, there's
no chasing to do; no protecting.
No tiny fingers searching for electrical outlets or
unwelcoming cats.
The floors are clean enough for who lives here.
Relax.
Have some wine. Listen to the silence.
Turn the tree lights on.
This is the life you have.
Put on some Tchaikovsky and wrap some presents.
What you have is more than most.
A peace of sorts despite what's lost
I put out of my mind the havoc of caring for small fingers
and toes.
I tell myself to enjoy this restful, this quiet repose
No tripping over plastic toys
Or piles of laundry from a messy boy
Only my own face reflected back from the bottom of my
merlot
You are watched over, I tell myself
In the tree's warm glow.

2.4.17
What I planted

Show me a life worth living
One not covered in grime and sweat
Or fur from a favored pet, now old and dying
Everything beloved destined to wilt
Treasured hands that will turn to silt and
Too soon be replaced the way that everything is replaced
The last steps through the threshold followed
Quickly by new steps in
The house emptied and then refilling, adding the next
stranger to the din
And it will be his turn to plant trees in the lawn, making it
his instead of mine
All that I made no longer pertaining to me
Nothing, in fact, giving witness to my useless love
The years of it that I rubbed over everything I thought
would always matter
This life fruitless like the millions of others
Passing with no remnant
Not even a lone lily
To attest that once it was my hands
That laid it there.

11.3.17
The Calling

I pull songs from my apron pockets
They come from every place I've ever been
From porches, gardens, mailboxes—I give them to the
wind
The bathing dishes, the thirsty flowers, I unload tune after
tune—
Why did God give me all of these songs
When I cannot give them to you?

I have dabs of color on my paintbrushes ready
Purple-bellied clouds scooting steady down an avenue of
sky
Hog's bristle arching with laden sigh
The shivering blue underbrush, the cardamom cry
Of dogwood slick in the shadows
I trace the starlight with my eyes
And paint out my hunger for blue,
Why did God give me all of these colors
When I cannot give them to you?

What is a life given to longing?
It is no genuine pigment but a hue.
I sharpen my practice for a Calling
But I am unsure what I am being called to
What is calling for me, my sweet absent son,
As I call and call for you?

3.20.18
Asherman's

Afterwards they all sent letters, cards
And the women's pens—some nearly strangers—poured
out words their mouths had refused for years
I could see the smeared ink
And the man who had lost his first-born forty years ago
Wept silently at the table where our coffees turned cold in
their mugs.

It wasn't until after my twelfth miscarriage that I learned
about my own scarring
How it had held on to the parts of my babies that my womb
refused to let go:
Past placentas still pulsing with the heartbeats of children I
had lost
Tangled in the scarred webs that had pulled my womb
closed—
Nearly-sealed—with only one thin line of passage to the
one ovary
That gave us hope.
How many more losses before that would seal too?

It is a delicate affair—the removal of scar tissue
It took several procedures with healing time between each
But the doctors told me that there was hope that my womb
could heal.

Who sat with this man to tell him why his son had died?
Who asked him how it felt—asked him about his hopes, his
love,
All that he had lost?
Or the woman who wept into a card for the child she lost
nearly fifty years ago?
Who broke up the scar tissue piece by piece
With small safe spaces in between

So that these humans could heal the inner surfaces of their
own soft hearts
So that their unwilling mouths could work out the tightness
That clamped down on the unspeakable tenderness that
each child brings to their parents?

Part of me wanted to keep what was there, what remnants
remained as proof of life whose loss I could net yet
reconcile.
But it was not true life, what was left.
I was told that those remnants could grow into something
unchecked and harmful.

And as I counted backwards and looked up at the surgeon
who would heal me,
I thanked the Universe for giving me things so very
precious
That it had nearly killed me
to have to let go.

# Epilogue Poem

3.21.18
The Girl

I have turned into a pomegranate these last few months
Whose skin is stretched taut as labyrinths build themselves
once again inside me
Each new day she continues to grow
And it reminds me of you and of miracles.
I feel her and all of her circles and spheres
And think of all the ways I do not know you.
Her tiny pockets are already filling with eggs she won't
discover for decades
And I hold all of you close to me, lost, living, and yet-to-
be:
My complicated family
Tangled sweet
Cluster of pomegranate seeds
Bursting with everything
That I will never know about you
Though I have loved you and loved all of you
The best I could.